Minding
.HER
Business

Ivy Ejam

ISBN-13: 978-1519273031
ISBN-10: 1519273037

Dedication

This book is dedicated to every woman who dares to dream of a better life. The woman who has realized that enough is enough. The woman who for far too long, allowed life to mold how she feels but has realized it is how she feels that molds her life.

Today, she has discovered there is more to life. Today she has realized that what she receives in life is limited by what she feels she deserves. Today, she has decided she deserves a life full of joy, happiness, abundance, peace, financial security, and love.

IVY EJAM

TABLE OF CONTENTS

WHAT TO EXPECT

It is recommended to not use this book as a normal book that you would read from cover to cover (but if you'd like to, then by all means go for it). This book is meant to work more as a troubleshooter to help you overcome specific obstacles in your life. We all have different goals and ideas of what we call a "beautiful life". The writings here are meant to assist you in adopting the proper mindset needed to get what you desire most.

Through out this book you will find motivational texts, advice, a list of daily affirmations, manifestation guides, and short stories catered to motivating you to live a better life. This entails all topics; health, love, relationships, confidence, prosperity, knowledge, and personal development.

Knowledge truly is power so never take it for granted once you've gained new insight. It is just as divine as all other

IVY EJAM

matters of goodness as it is meant to enrich your life. Whatever you desire is yours to acquire so long as you believe and act in accordance to what you've learned.

That said, as you go through this book, try seeing it as doses of prescription medication. Don't just read when to take it and how many doses to take, you must actually take them in order to see results and improvement in your life. I'm excited to be a part of this journey with you and hope you truly apply what you'll be learning here.

1

SELF LOVE

THE FIRST STEP

In this section, we will go over how to acquire a mindset of self-love. In order to receive the best, you must feel that you deserve to receive it. This can be difficult to achieve if you yourself feel undeserving of things that make you happy. This is why loving yourself is the first step toward attracting a better life. If you're having issues with confidence, insecurity, and self-doubt, this is the chapter for you!

THE MINDSET

You can not put acquisition before desire. Desire is the driving force behind what you attract into your life. We desire what we feel we deserve, and what we feel we deserve has everything to do with who we think we are.

Just as a poor man would never step foot into an establishment where he knows he cannot afford the service, a person who thinks low of themselves would never aspire to acquire circumstance of high quality as they feel they're undeserving. However, it is the rich man that treads any ground with confidence, knowing his footsteps are worthy of touching all grounds equal to his quality worth.

Becoming rich in love is synonymous to becoming rich in your vibrational net worth. The more it grows, so does your capacity to receive. So the question is, who do you think you are? Well, I will be the first to tell you who you're not. You're not someone who deserves to live life in misery. You are not someone that should wake up every morning dreading another day that she has to go to a job she doesn't like, making money that's not enough, and surrounded by those who don't inspire her to be her best self.

You may not know this, but you are much more capable of attaining greatness than you're currently aware. As I've previously stated, the fact that you're reading this book right now is proof that a part of you knows that it's time for a major change. A part of you is truly tired of the life you currently live and is ready to make major moves in order to make your dreams a reality.

First, repeat the words below:

- I AM -

A QUEEN

because I

Govern my reality
Rule my happiness
Lead my ambitions

We are all queens because we have the ability to make changes in our lives so long as we are aware that we can.

If you look back at your life, try to recall moments in your life where you've actually acquired something that you desired. Was it not because you actually wanted it to happen? Now try to recall moments in your life where you required a rather unfortunate circumstance. If you think hard enough, was it because you had a fear of that thing coming to fruition?

All things we encounter in our lives truly are by no accident. The issue is, because we are mostly unaware of how effective our thoughts are toward our reality, we allow life to kick us in the butt. Not only have we been unaware of the effects of our thoughts, but our thoughts themselves have the tendency to run rampant in our minds.

What you put your thoughts and focus toward a majority of the time inevitably manifests in your life. You may have heard of this concept from the popular book titled "The Secret" - well it's true! The sooner you start catching the thoughts and impressions that you have about yourself over and over again, the quicker you can begin to change this.

Not only do your thoughts have power, but the words you speak do as well. One of the major things that have helped me greatly towards personal development are affirmations. Affirmations are essentially proclamations that you speak over your life. Since you are what you believe, and you receive what you desire, that means that you speak things into existence by stating them as if they truly are.

For example, repeat these affirmations:

I am loved
I am whole
I am impeccable
I am highly capable
I am beautiful
I am important

I am abundant
I am sufficient
I am ENOUGH

Didn't that feel good? Even if you are having a hard time believing those words right now, just by simply stating them you are speaking those truths into existence in your life. As often as you speak those words and encompass yourself in thoughts of self-love, you will begin to feel those words as truths in your life.

NOTE: Through out this book, at the end of select sections, you will be presented with a list of helpful affirmations that should assist you in acquiring your desired mindset.

MONITOR YOUR THOUGHTS
BECOME SO POSITIVE THAT NEGATIVITY MAKES YOU SICK

Okay, so now that you understand the basic concept of "thoughts create my reality", the next step is to tame your thoughts.

Some time ago, before my life truly turned around, I would say my thoughts were easily 80-90% negative with rare positivity. Now you may say that's a lot, but what we don't realize is what actually counts as a negative thought. Negative thoughts don't just come in the form of "I can't do this" or "I'll never make enough money", but also in the form of "I'm still here because …" or "If it wasn't for XYZ I'd be rich by now". In other words, rather than giving attention to what I wanted to see happen, I gave attention to that which already was.

Now that I live on my own, without any negative influences, being immersed in positive thoughts has become so dominant within my being that negativity makes me sick. Yes, at times even physically. You see, the more you surround yourself with positive thoughts and feelings, the more you begin to elevate your spiritual vibrational atmosphere.

Metaphorically speaking:
If low vibrations were the ground, higher vibrations would be up in the sky where the atmospheric pressure decreases the higher up you go.

When a negative thought envelopes your mind at a "higher altitude", it begins to bring you down near the ground where pressure is higher. Now you can imagine, more pressure added to a being who has been dwelling in a low pressure atmosphere (higher up) for so long will become very uncomfortable. It will be noticeable, you will not like it, and you should do everything in your power to get rid of it!

This is why when you begin to attain success and your peers do not, they no longer become your peers. Places you used to go will change, the way you speak and treat others will change. You will almost feel alienated for a while until you find your new vibrational family up in the sky (i.e. like-minded individuals).

Challenge

I challenge you to a 24hr monitoring of your thoughts. Anytime you think of a negative thought or anytime someone says something negative to you, write it down. Whenever a positive thought crosses your mind, write that down as well. This is to give you an idea of your daily thought patterns. At the end of the day, examine the thought patterns you wrote down.

Do you worry about bills every time you're about to open the mail? Why is that so? You know bills are going to come every month so what is the point of fearing the inevitable? Have you tried being grateful instead that even though you have bills to pay every month, you're somehow able to pay them? Have you ever just said, "I'm thankful that I'm able to pay my bills, no matter how high the amount"?

When you desire to buy a designer bag that's a bit above your pay grade, do you find yourself saying "I don't have enough money for that."? Have you instead tried saying "Although I have the money to pay for that if I wanted to, I'd rather spend it on something else". Because truth be told, you most likely do have the money for it but instead use it to pay for something more important.

Do you check your balance often just to see how low your balance is? Have you instead tried limiting the amount of times you check your balance and affirming to yourself "I'm thankful that I have enough money in my account to buy the things that I need."?

I guarantee you that if you begin to change your daily thought patterns you will begin to see an imminent change in the flow of your income and other areas of your life.

WANT CHANGE?
DON'T JUST SAY IT, SEE IT!
While it is very important to affirm where you want to be as if you already are, speaking just the words will not be enough to get you there.

Words alone are powerless if they are not accompanied by feeling and intent. Even those who are deaf and mute are still able feel and put together a matter of thought. Those thoughts accompanied by feeling are what you should truly focus on when you affirm your desires daily. Focus on every word that proceeds out of your mouth and say it with the power given to you knowing that there is authority behind your proclamations. Believe in every word as if you are merely stating a fact!

The path to attracting abundance isn't a mental diet one undergoes for a while until the desired goal is reached, it is a lifestyle. Shifting ones consciousness into a state of **"I AM ABUNDANT"** and **"I AM IN CONTROL"** doesn't happen overnight, and must be felt from within you as well as seen within your mind.

Just as it's easy for you to see yourself waking up every morning to go to work, drive in traffic, sit at a 9-5 desk, and come home - you should see yourself in your desired reality as if it's already there. Consider this, the universe cannot differentiate between a real memory or a fabricated one. It goes on how you felt and reacted as a result of visual experience. That in mind, haven't you at times confused a dream or a thought in your head with reality and asked yourself...

"Wait, did that actually happen or did I imagine that?"

Simple answer, it doesn't matter! If you can **SAY IT, SEE IT, FEEL IT,** and **BE IT,** then **IT** truly **BECOMES.**

DAILY AFFIRMATION

I AM IN
CONTROL
OF MY REALITY

AFFIRMATIONS
FOR A POSITIVE MINDSET & BEING IN CONTROL

I am in control of my reality

I am capable of attracting anything I want

I deserve happiness

I am able to see my desired reality clearly

I only think positive thoughts

I am surrounded by positivity

I am limitless

I am the solution to all of my problems

CONFIDENCE

So, who are you? I will ask this question a lot through out this chapter as it is very important. If you haven't heard, it is my pleasure to be the first to tell you:

Whoever you think you are, or think you aren't, you're right - so think positively of yourself!

Do any of these phrases sound familiar to you?

"I'm so lazy"
"Oh gosh, I can't believe I didn't understand that, I'm so stupid"
"I'm so bad with managing money"
"I'm just not great at looking my best"
"I'm never going to be as pretty or slim as she is"
"I'm just not capable of doing that"

Your words are so very powerful my dear! If you want to become a better you, you need to start speaking to yourself as if you are speaking to your idol.

One highly effective way to boost your confidence is to practice visual affirmations by using a mirror. If you're more of a visual person, this technique can really assist you in seeing yourself as you desire to be.

Simply get yourself all prettied up, nice outfit, make your hair presentable and stand in front of a mirror. (try to do this when you're on your way out). Now as you look at the person in the mirror, pretend for a moment that she is not you. Imagine that this person is someone you've heard about through the grapevine. Just as you may know a few things about a celebrity, start to tell the story of this person as if you're merely stating a fact. Ask yourself questions and answer them how you desire to see her.

Here are a few ideas of questions to ask the woman in the mirror:

- What kind of car does she drive?
- What does her wardrobe look like?
- Who is she dating and what does he look like?
- Is he successful too?
- Does she own her own business?
- What's her net worth?
- Who's in her circle of friends?
- What does she like to do in her spare time?
- Does she like to exercise?
- What does a typical meal for her look like?
- What's her energy like, is she fun to be around?

Make sure as you're answering these questions that you're smiling with a proud, confident, stance.

This is powerful because the moment you do that, you put out vibrations that affect how others see you the moment they see you. Don't believe it? Try it for yourself. I realized this worked the moment I started to love how my body appeared in the mirror. I saw that woman in the mirror and would say, "damn, I look good!". Ever since then, I've started to receive compliments from women specifically about my body whenever I would go out.

This is also very important for those who are currently in a relationship and may start feeling unattractive or like their partner is losing interest. When you start to feel that way, get in front of a mirror and tell your significant other what you want them to see by seeing it yourself. Get to it - right now! "Mirror mirror on the wall, who is this fine Goddess I see before me!" Do this as often as you need it.

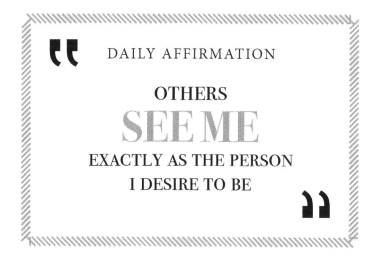

DAILY AFFIRMATION

OTHERS

SEE ME

**EXACTLY AS THE PERSON
I DESIRE TO BE**

THE IMPORTANCE OF STYLE

ADDRESS THE WAY YOU DRESS

It should be understood that you are your brand identity package. First impressions aren't just psychological, they're metaphysical. Ever hear the expression fake it till you make it? Well in this case, the universe does not see it as "faking" it. We are constantly picking up information about those around us consciously and intuitively. With that in mind, **whoever** you think you are or think you aren't, you're right.

We are all familiar with the feeling we get when we look our best. Not only do we exude confidence, but the very thing that inspired us to spend the time out of our day to look our best was indeed a love we had for ourselves at the moment that said "I'm worth it". As you grow to learn these secrets of success and life in general, you'll learn that time is an invaluable currency that should be spent wisely, both physically and in thought!

How you treat yourself ultimately tells others how to treat you, and the easiest way to express that is with your presentation. I don't have to be the one to tell you that first impressions matter, but what matters even more is how you feel about the impression that you're giving out.

If you are a woman who sees herself as a woman not worthy of the finer things, the universe will say "your wish is my command". That thought will perpetuate a vibration that others will pick up, whether they want to or not, and the subsequent events that follow will heed the desired result - "you're not worth it". On the other hand, when you begin to truly love yourself and show it by taking care of yourself, the reactions from people around you **will** begin to change.

This must be addressed. You externalize the impressions you have about yourself, so if you truly want to start making moves and changes in your life, ask yourself first what story you're telling others with your style.

Now, anyone can exude confidence and sophistication without buying expensive brand clothing. It's not the cost of the clothing that defines your worth, it's how you assemble the ensemble in a way that best makes you FEEL like a million bucks.

If you're not feeling like you're a woman on a mission by the time you've gotten all dressed up and ready, then tweak and change something until you do. Sorry fellas, she's gonna be a couple more minutes. From personal experience, the moment I started to dress in a way that I felt resonated with how I felt about myself, was the moment I started walking with my head held high.

Remind yourself that you are a woman that is worth getting to know. You are a woman that knows what she wants out of life and knows her worth. You are a woman that likes to take care of herself because she loves herself enough to know she deserves to be taken care of. Externalize the impression of "I'm worth it" - because trust me, you are.

This of course doesn't just end with how you look but also how you walk, speak, smile, and treat others. All of these actions work in agreement with one main vibration stemming from the impressions you have about YOURSELF. Figure that out first - then fix it. You get in life what you feel you deserve, so start realizing today that you deserve the very best and all the happiness in this world.

DAILY REMINDER

YOUR
CONFIDENCE
& STYLE IS YOUR COVER LETTER TO THE RESUME OF YOUR LIFE AS A GODDESS

POSTURE & COUNTENANCE .

WHAT'S THE POINT OF HAVING THAT PRETTY FACE IF IT'S ALWAYS FACING THE FLOOR, DARLING?

A stranger doesn't have to be a psychologist to gauge when someone they meet is insecure about themselves. Before we formerly introduce ourselves to someone new, we issue an introduction visually through our actions. Our stride is undoubtedly our cover letter and our facial expression is our "Dear Sir/Madam".

How do you walk when you're strutting down the street? Are your shoulders back or are you slouched? What does your facial expression say about your self-impression? Do you wear a well-rested and confident smile, or do you look like you don't want to be out in public and just want to go home?

Our body has the tendency to create a very open posture based on what we are willing to receive. To that respect, if your posture is exuding a message of "Don't come close!", you are potentially shooing away a lot of good opportunities to meet some great people!

As I've often mentioned, how you feel about yourself is a key factor in what you receive in your life. You get what you feel you deserve, and if you don't feel you deserve the best, you will not receive the best. It really is as simple as that. To that regard, when you love and have the utmost respect for yourself, you should exude that in every angle of your life.

You never know who you're going to meet, and **when** you're going to meet them. It can be at a grocery store, pumping gas, or at the post office. That said, try as much as possible to be aware of the signals you're sending out on a daily basis. Treat every outing experience as if you're interviewing for a job because you essentially are. If you ever truly want anything great to happen in your life, they're most likely going to happen through the connections you make. That said, it's best to make as many as you possibly can!

"I KEEP MY HEAD HELD HIGH TO KEEP MY CROWN FROM FALLING DOWN"

If you feel this might be you and are in need of a little help, try out this exercise.
(It may seem a little silly, but if you can't be a little silly in front of yourself, how can you expect to be a little confident in front of other people?)

Get all dressed up, wear something nice, and if you like (not mandatory) put on some heels. Just make sure you are looking your best. Get in front of the nearest full body mirror and take a good look.

1. **Turn to the side and examine your shoulders while you are in a resting stance.**
   Are you slouching? Try pushing them to the back. Straight enough that the side of your shoulders run parallel to side of your ribs.

2. **Make sure that your head is up and your neck is back.**
   Turn your chin up so that it runs parallel to the floor, and your neck should be aligned with your shoulders. Not only is good posture good for presentation, but it also prevents joint and back issues in the future.

3. **Examine your resting face**
   This is actually something I've "suffered" from and still battle on from time to time. I display something commonly known as "B*tchy resting face." I can only speak for me, but I notice this typically happens when I'm either tired, bored, or really am not paying much attention to my surroundings.

We don't really realize just how impactful something as simple as your countenance can be toward your approachability - but it is! If you want to venture out with a more approachable demeanor, I've found that it helps to envelope your mind in positive thought. Just like when you're thinking about someone you really like and just happen to start smiling, you can consciously apply that circumstance to your everyday habits.

Encompass your mind in your future goals, or things that make you happy. Have in your mind that "I am a beautiful woman that is going great places in my life!". Not only is this good for your countenance, but it does wonders for your vibrations.

Venture out like you're on a mission to let everyone who comes in contact with you see that you're someone worth getting to know. Figure out the impression you want to send out, affirm it within you, then STRUT!

DAILY AFFIRMATION

I AM NATURALLY

CONFIDENT

OUTGOING, FRIENDLY, &
OPEN

SEX APPEAL

....

HOW TO FEEL ATTRACTIVE

To be clear, there are **many** ways to display confidence and sex appeal and it has a lot to do with how you FEEL. A true sexy woman is one that can make anything she wears look attractive. She acquires desirability with the smile she wears as she walks with a confident sultry look in her eyes.

A true confident woman garners attractive quality when she knows she has a deep interesting secret buried deep that only those worthy enough get to hear. Her secret is that she has a personality to die for and can sustain your attention for aeons. A true desirable woman is one that has you so in awe of her presence, that to a man, she becomes an expedition to embark rather than a task to check off his list.

Remember ladies, we all pretty much look the same underneath our clothes, there will never be any big surprise there. What is really intriguing is how you choose to wrap your present and externalize how you feel about yourself by how you put together your ensemble and how you feel wearing it.

It seems in todays society, promiscuity or appearing promiscuous has become more celebrated and portrayed as a form of female empowerment and being reserved pegs you as either boring, inexperienced, or may make you feel undesirable.
If you're in this boat right now and want to feel sexy again without compromising your morale, read on.

As it is true that you should dress to make yourself feel good, there will always be another factor - the desire to attract a partner and feel sexy and desirable to a man.

Appeal is defined as "the power or ability to attract, interest, amuse, or stimulate the mind or emotions". Although men are very visual creatures, their true interest lies in a woman who can challenge them. To restate, a man likes to be challenged, not a woman who is a challenge. Drama and bad attitude is not and never will be cute. "Lady lumps" may be a nice distraction to dart a mans eyes your way, but what lasts longer is what **stimulates the mind.**

To put things in perspective, consider this:

Imagine you are sitting at a table full of cards that are assigned to each woman who sits there. Each card has something special and unique on it that only they know. Imagine there are men sitting on the other side of the table who also have their own cards. Now, imagine some women begin to turn over their cards to draw attention from the men across the table. The men become instantly drawn to the women who have decided to turn over their cards, see bright red colors, maybe some glitter, interesting shapes, etc. They begin to talk to the women more about the cards given what they've just seen.

Then there's you. You notice how pretty everyone else's cards are and see how interested the men begin to become in that. You start to question if yours is even special. I mean, why should you keep hiding what you have if it's great, right? Those women showed theirs knowing they have something good, and the men seem to be very interested. If I'm proud in what I have, shouldn't I show it?

SEXINESS ISN'T HOW YOU LOOK, IT'S HOW YOU FEEL.

Don't be so quick to compromise your values by turning over that card - here is what you do! Imagine, instead of turning over your card, you keep it concealed. You applaud the women down the table for their bravery, and continue to leave your card down. You smile and agree with the men across the table, and say

"oh yes, what that woman has is stunning!"

But now, the men begin to wonder. Why is that woman smiling? She's got her head held high and a smile on her face. She doesn't wince at the women who've shown their cards, and she refuses to show us what she has.

Imagine suddenly all the men that were looking at the other women's cards begin to look in your direction. They wonder what makes you smile and what you've got hidden. They try to put two and two together, wondering, if this woman can look at the beauty of these women's cards without feeling like hers is less superior, then she must have something better!

So, now there's something about you that becomes appealing and desirable. The men now begin to ask YOU questions & because they have not seen what's on your card, they instead try to figure you out based on what they've just observed through your **character**. They want to see what makes you happy, and confident. These thoughts begin to envelope so abundantly in their minds that they shortly after begin to ignore what they just saw down the table from the other women.

Now here's the real kicker. The more those women reveal what's on their card, the more your conceal becomes more intriguing. Why? Well because what value lies in something that has been so easily overturned? It may attract attention for a season, but we are not to be women of temporary amusement!

We are worth more than that, and men are not stupid. They know which women to wife and which women will not keep them mentally stimulated. So the next time you see a woman in reality or on TV making you feel like less of a woman because you're not doing what they're doing - remember this. Your only competition is the woman in the mirror, and last time you checked, she's got an amazing card.

Just smile, keep your head high, don't envy the women who don't look as you do, and remember that you too have something special. So special in fact that you refuse to reveal it to just any Tom, Rick, Ramone or Tyrone. That is the sexiest most empowering thing you could do!

DAILY AFFIRMATION

I ALWAYS
EXEMPLIFY
CONFIDENCE,
SOPHISTICATION,
KINDNESS & CLASS

AFFIRMATIONS
FOR SEX APPEAL, CONFIDENCE, & ATTRACTION

I am confident

I am very sexy

I am incredibly beautiful

I am worth getting to know

I am respected

I am incredibly attractive

I attract those who I am attracted to

I love the way I look

I exude sex appeal

My body is incredible

My body is sexy

Men are intrigued by me

Men find me irresistible

My confidence shows

I am grateful for my confidence

I am thankful for my body

My smile is irresistible

I am approachable

*My {**body part**} is my best feature*

2

WEALTH & PROSPERITY

In this chapter we will go over the good stuff, acquiring a wealthy mindset! This is something many desire the most but don't know the first steps to begin. If you currently find yourself in a job you don't like, making money that's not enough, and desire to live a life full of purpose and financial security, then read on!

THE MINDSET

MONEY IS A SOURCE ENERGY

If you desire to have a more abundant life, you should understand the true purpose behind currency in order to acquire it. Money is an energy that flows just as the rivers do. It allows ideas to manifest into material and thoughts to become action. It only has value when it moves from hand to hand.

This means that the desire to have money only to hoard money can actually prolong the acquisition of wealth. The desire to be rich only to pile on the dollars is the same as preventing another from experiencing the benefits of a flowing stream. If the river does not flow, it can not perform its duty around the world to cleanse, refresh, provide food, transport, generate electricity and many other benefits.

As mentioned in the "Self-Love" chapter, you get in life what you truly feel you deserve. In this case, if you don't feel you're worthy of have having a financially abundant life, you will find difficulty in receiving that.

The absolute truth is that you're entitled to abundance as a co-creator. If you desire to make your dreams a reality by turning your thoughts into tangible form, money is an energy that has been set in place to perform that very action. That said, you have every right to receive resources necessary to manifest your hearts desires, be it $5 or $10 million.

DAILY AFFIRMATION

MONEY
FLOWS TO ME
EFFORTLESSLY,
ABUNDANTLY, &
WILLINGLY

MONEY IS POWERLESS WITHOUT YOU

Money is not a poor mans problem, it is his mindset and ideas toward money. If you were to receive it without mastering it & understanding its intended purpose, it will not solve all of your problems and can thwart you on your journey to self-mastery.

Try imaging money as an entity that desires to be used in order to grow in value - because it is. The paper itself has absolutely no value until it is exchanged for a product, service, or thought. The more focus you give to money as merely stacks that you wish to collect, the more you move away from its intended purpose which will make money run away from you.

Imagine money as the popular pretty girl in high school. Every guy wants to date her but most don't have the courage to approach her because they feel she's out of their league. The ones that do pursue her are the ones who feel they too have worth and know that if they were to date, he would add value to her status, and she would add value to his.

If you wish to increase your monetary wealth, think of the value you're giving to it by what you plan on doing with it. Money would have no choice but to flock to you as both of your purposes would be in alignment.

MONEY IS TRANSFERABLE FAVOR

As I've mentioned many times before, money has the ability to transform thoughts into action and ideas into physical form. However, this is something that is often easily forgotten at the very first acquisition of any small amount of wealth. We tend to want to spend it on things that we wouldn't have when we didn't have the money. I was guilty of this! As it is nice to enjoy what you've worked hard for, it is much sweeter to use your new income source to **scale up** your efforts.

We're all aware of the time and effort it takes for fruits and vegetables to grow. Months, some YEARS of hard labor until finally the harvest! Now, you can take that time to indulge in what you've just grown, or you can take some of the seeds from your fruits and plant back into the soil.

It is no accident that for every fruit or vegetable you grow you reap more seeds than you started out with. Replication and abundance is in our nature. That said, once you've achieved your first amount of fruit, the next harvest should not be for minuscule profits. You have more seeds this time, use it to scale up your returns. Sow a portion of your money back into your business or use it to start up a second one. However, this time when you sow again, instead of struggling & waiting years for returns, use money as favor to skip the line and accelerate your progress.

One good way to do this is to set aside a certain portion of your monthly income aside for side projects. You can also be smart with your money by using it to replace a job. If you know that you have to work a certain amount of hours per day toward a certain aspect of your business, pay someone else to do it for you so you can focus on something else. Always remember this important benefit of money. Use it for its intended purpose. Desire it for its intended use.

AFFIRMATIONS
FOR ATTRACTING MONEY

I deserve financial abundance

I am financially abundant

I never lack money

I am financially secure

I receive what I need when I need

I always have more money that I realize

Money comes to me from various sources

Money is always available to me the exact time that I need

My resources are unlimited

My bank account is never low

Money flows to me willingly

Money flows to me abundantly

Money flows to me effortlessly

Money desires to be used by me

Financial security brings me joy

I am able to pay for whatever I want

My funds are endless

THE IMPORTANCE OF GIVING

FREELY YOU GIVE, FREELY SHALL YOU RECEIVE

Now that we've gone over the purpose of currency and the proper mindset to have with regards to receiving, it is also important for us to understand the importance of giving.

Like all forms energy, in order to flow it must be released. The moment money moves from one hand to another, its purpose is being fulfilled and goodness continues to flow.

That considered, it's important to realize that when we give money from the goodness of our heart, it is to be celebrated. When you give, you not only give value to the dollar but you are also blessing another with your contribution. Think of the ripple-effect of events that will transpire from your simple act of kindness. Just as money is drawn to you to fulfill your purposes and hearts desires, when you allow currency to circulate, you are assisting in the manifestation of another's desires as well.

If you desire to have a more fulfilling abundant life, give with joy knowing that you are blessing someone else and giving value to the dollar. When you're out shopping, don't bring out your wallet with a heavy heart, fear, and the thought of you having less money. We never truly have "less money", only money that is currently in the hands of another. It is favor being transferred, and when it is our time to need the favor, money will come to us as well.

You also tell the universe how you easily you will receive that abundance by how tight you hold onto what you currently have. As what we receive is based on intent and focus, if your focus is on gathering money with no intent to use it to manifest anything of purpose, you will have a tough time receiving. That said, you essentially demonstrate your intentions through your current habits. You get more of that which makes you happy, and so if giving to others freely gives you joy, and if currency has the intent of being given freely and abundantly to others, guess where it will want to go?

Some lose sight of this and wonder why their flow of income hasn't increased because they try so hard to keep as much money in the bank as possible. You must see your financial flow as a pipe that is expanding, not a vault that is growing! As your pipe grows, your account balance may seem like it is increasing, when in fact, it is actually your income and spending that is expanding.

Example

Gain $10,000, spend $5,000 out of that, you still have $5,000 left. Gain $20,000, spend $12,000, and you have $8,000 left again. This does not mean your wealth is not increasing by much. What it does mean is that your wealth is being utilized for a purpose that demands more money and so your pipe expands to accommodate.

Now as I tell you this, make no mistake that I am implying that you go to the nearest stranger and give them all of your heard earned dollars. Whatever you give, give joyfully and willingly. You are not obligated to be charitable, but when you do feel the desire to be so, it should come from the goodness of your heart without expecting anything return.

I know, I know, I just said freely we give, freely we receive. However, your intent to give should not come with a hidden agenda to receive. Remember this when I say, give for the joy of blessing another! You are not only giving value to the dollar, but also allowing someone else's purpose to be fulfilled! Never forget this, and do only give when you truly feel lead to give from a place of happiness. When you give with joy, you will receive with joy.

GIVE FOR THE JOY OF BLESSING ANOTHER. LET NOT YOUR INTENTION COME FROM REAPING REWARDS.

AFFIRMATIONS
FOR GIVING & RECEIVING

I enjoy giving

I am a generous individual

Giving makes me happy

I am grateful for the ability that I have to give

I am grateful for the lives I affect positively through my giving

I am grateful for the wealth that I've attained

I bless others with my giving

I am thankful for the opportunity to give

My flow of wealth is expanding

I welcome opportunities to give

I welcome opportunities to bless others

I receive easily and abundantly

I am grateful for my increase in income

SUCCESS

....

DEFINING SUCCESS

Before you can achieve success in your life, you must define what success means to you. This is actually something that I had to come to terms with before starting my blog on Instagram.

I had always thought that my achievements were insignificant in the eyes of the masses who commonly look to millionaires for advice on how to be successful. I quickly found that I was wrong in this regard as I began writing out the things I had learned about life.

I learned the true definition of success is in acquiring exactly what you desire - no matter how big or small. The day that I **consciously** decided I wanted something and received it was the day my eyes were truly opened. I had undeniably succeeded in achieving something that was seemingly impossible for me to attain at the time. I defined the lifestyle that I wanted to acquire and made that into a reality.

"I WANT A LIFE AS BEAUTIFUL AS I AM"

Beauty is subjective, so not everyone's definition of a beautiful life will be the same. For some its the luxury, glamour and expensive things. For others its a small dream home over seas with a big family. Or perhaps having no home is your definition of a beautiful life and you desire to travel from country to country experiencing the world. Whatever you desire your reality to be, just know there is no right or wrong as to what defines a beautiful life. As long as it brings you joy, it is a life worth living.

The best way to achieve your beautiful life is to become a vibrational match to those desires. Begin to define your idea of a beautiful life by identifying the beauty within you. Get to know you by understanding your likes and dislikes. Whatever you've found that you love about yourself you will most likely want to magnify and externalize that in your life. Whatever excites your spirit when you think about it, hold on to it and begin to carve out what your ideal life style would be.

Try painting a mental picture by putting together a vision board of a lifestyle you'd like to see become a reality. Tweak it & add photos till it FEELS right. If you've found that you've got a smile on your face as you're putting these visuals together, keep going!

It also helps to acknowledge the beauty in your current lifestyle and to show gratitude towards that. Don't think about the aspects of your life that you don't like, and really begin to pay attention to the aspects of your life that bring you happiness and make you feel at peace.

"I WOULD RATHER BELIEVE IN ACHIEVING GREATNESS AND BE WRONG, THAN DOUBT THE POSSIBILITY & BE RIGHT"

TAKE MORE RISKS

Two words that literally changed my life - "Why not". If you truly want to see great change in your life it involves taking great risks. The reason you know when you're soon to make a life changing decision is when it scares you. Considering doing what you've always done keeps you where you currently are, it's only when you've disturbed the balance of your daily ritual do you begin to graze the surface of transfiguration.

Not doing, not trying, not risking, not pursuing will always bring you one result - not achieving. When you realize you have nothing to lose by breaking out of your box of conformity and at least trying, the decision should be simple.

Success doesn't come from the element of persistence alone, but from persistently pushing past the norms of which you currently stand. The greater the risk the greater the reward. If you desire to be in a position greater than where you are, you have to be willing to do something greater than what you currently do.

Decide today that you are going to push fear aside and ask yourself "why not?" more often. About 99% of the time there is no explanation great enough to prevent you from at least trying. Most of the time, the only TRUE thing stopping us is our ego. If I don't make it, what will others say, what will they think? You will survive my dear.

Your journey to success is yours to enjoy and not for onlookers who examine you from a distance to see whether you will win or fail. The best part of the journey is in the failures so if you win or fail, it is still a win-win. Failures only make the win feel oh-so-sweet. Try so you can fail. Believe so you can achieve. Doubt, and you'll be left out.

"WHEN SMALL THINGS FAIL IN MULTITUDE, GREATER THINGS ARE SUCCEEDING IN MAGNITUDE."

Experiencing constant failure is inevitable however it is also incredibly valuable. If you truly wish to acquire a magnitude of success, you must realize that preparation must ensue for such a massive acquisition. Each failure experienced may not seem like a "little thing" to you at the time, but it's only when you've attained the BIG success do you realize how small that failure was in comparison.

Your best education can come from experience, and the only way you're going to learn anything valuable is from experiences where you didn't get what you expected. If we got everything right on the first try, we would not know the exact factors that caused it to succeed. More importantly, there would be no growth from that point on considering you did something which resulted in you getting something. Most likely, you will repeat the same process again with **no change** in order to get the same results. However, your measure of growth would be non-existent as you have no failure to compare it to.

If you're familiar with marketing, you would know that it takes many failures in order to create a good campaign. There are a lot of factors involved, and the only way for you to create the highest converting campaign is to know what doesn't work so you can do the opposite of that.

So **DO IT**, and fail. Don't know the cause? Try again, fail again. Compare the two and see the common denominator. Still unsure? Try again, change a few things, fail again. See the common denominator between the three. Keep going, changing, tweaking, and most importantly, keep trying. The more failures you encounter, the more clarity you receive and ammunition you gain to create something **UNSINKABLE**.

TRY MORE so you can FAIL MORE. You'll be glad you did. Keep doing it until you hit a breakthrough. Otherwise, if you quit before you've hit that magnitude, you'll just be left with a lot of unanswered questions.

BE IN THE BUSINESS OF MINDING YOUR OWN

The entire theme of my Instagram was inspired by a principle that I very much still live by till today. Simply put, I learned the key to my own success was in minding my business. The moment I stopped announcing what I was going to do and simply did it, was the moment I began to see progress in my life. Family members may feel they are protecting you from failures that they've encountered in their lives, but they don't realize they are subjecting you to the ultimate failure of simply not trying.

Not to mention not all "blood" would be willing to give you a transfusion when you truly need it. Blood may be thicker than water, but when it stains, it is much harder to get out. In short, sometimes it is the next of kin that wish you the worst. Your closest friends may seem like your number 1 fans, but in actuality, most of them have absolutely no desire to see you excel higher then they have or ever will be. Onlookers will try to weigh in on your goals when it is simply none of their business as to what will make you happy.

Now, I'm not suggesting you go about life constantly looking over your shoulder for someone to betray you. What I am saying is that if you truly want to get from point A to Z, do it for you. Do it because you want to prove to yourself that you're more than the insecurities you may have adopted from other peoples opinions. Do it because you have a desire to become the best version of you, and only you know what a better version of you looks like. Let others discover the new you once you've finally gotten there. Let them see to believe rather than doubt to count you out.

If you are so incredibly excited about your goals and your plans for the future, only share it with those who live in the same vibrational gated community as you. Don't let those who don't even live on the same street try to tell you what color to paint your house or that your grass is too green.

DAILY AFFIRMATION

SUCCESS
IS INEVITABLE FOR ME BECAUSE I BELIEVE SO WITH EVERY FIBER OF MY BEING

AFFIRMATIONS
FOR A SUCCESS MINDSET

I am very successful

I achieve success

I am a success

Success is inevitable for me

Success is drawn to me

My actions are in alignment with hearts desires

I'm a risk taker

I am capable

I am unstoppable

I overcome obstacles with ease

I am a strong-willed individual

3

RELATION-SHIPS

In this chapter, we will go over the importance of different relationships and how to attract each type into your life. This chapter is ideal for anyone who is currently seeking a relationship, business partnerships, like-minded individuals, or if you're simply dealing with relationship issues.

FRIENDSHIPS

As we aspire to manifest success in all areas of our lives, let us not forget the invaluable asset of our friendships. Not only is networking great for accelerating your success, but it is also essential for vibrational resonance.

Striking a tuning fork and moving it closely to another tuning fork causes the fork that was once still to now vibrate at a similar frequency. This process is called forced vibration and when the vibration of the second fork finally matches that of the original fork, it is called resonance.

This happens far more often than we realize and should be utilized more to create our desired reality. Given that our thoughts vibrate as well, our mindsets, actions, and thus, vibrations do affect those we constantly associate with and vise versa.

The moment I began connecting with such successful, motivational, & passionate entrepreneurs on Instagram was the moment my hustle went into overdrive. It doesn't matter the distance between you, so long as words and ideas are exchanged, energy is being received. Your vibrations will have no choice but to assimilate. The more you do so, this will inevitably change your habits.

In this day and age, there is no excuse not to find some-one out there that has the same visions and goals as you. But don't just stop at associating with those who currently reside at your mindset, but also exceed your current mindset. If your goal is to be a millionaire, put your thoughts and intents out there to find more millionaires that you can resonate with.

DAILY AFFIRMATION

I AM SURROUNDED BY LIKE-MINDED, POSITIVE, & SUPPORTIVE INDIVIDUALS

HOW TO ATTRACT BETTER RELATIONSHIPS

Investing in the connections you make is truly a rewarding and vital element toward getting where you want to be in life. As long as you know who you are and what you want, this new in-ner circle can be drawn to you and you to it. You only have to be aware and ask of this.

The way to truly do this is to become a vibrational match to your desired connection. This means turning on the mindset of that which you wish to attract. You don't have to become a millionaire to align with the mindset of a millionaire, but you must align with the mindset of a millionaire in order to become one. To that degree, you can start coming into alignment with your desired vibrations now.

1. Define your vibration

Who are you and who do you want to attract? If you've found that your current friendships don't reflect who you are, it may be a good idea to examine the energy you're currently giving off.

2. Amplify your vibration

The best way to do this is to express gratitude and acknowledgment toward qualities that you'd like to bring forth. If you'd like to be around more goal driven individuals, amplify that part about yourself. Focus on your goals more and make that part about you a habit. If you'd like to be around more health conscious people, become more health conscious. If you already are, then acknowledge that part about you and express gratitude toward it. Affirm who you are and express pride toward that.

3. Get out there!

Join a community, online or offline. Start going to some events, or reach out - this is key! At times we may feel since the universe is so great at brining us what we want, we don't have to do much work for things to happen. There is no rule against meeting the universe halfway, actually, it is encouraged. If you see someone you'd like to get to know, reach out to them. You'd be surprised at how receptive they will be to your invitation.

AFFIRMATIONS
FOR ATTRACTING BETTER RELATIONSHIPS

I am a positive & driven individual

I am proud of who I am and who I am becoming

I am surrounded by like-minded individuals

I attract positive influences into my life

I am a person worth getting to know

I benefit from my friends, and my friends benefit from me

I am confident in myself

I am grateful for who I am

I deserve fulfilling relationships

My connections make me happy

My connections motivate me to do my best

My friendships reflect the person I want to become

My friends are encouraging individuals

My connections uplift and motivate me

My friendships give me joy

I am grateful for the positive influences in my life

ATTRACTING LOVE

At the risk of beating a dead horse here, loving yourself, again, is the most important element to attracting a LOVING romantic relationship. How can you expect to attract a partner that loves all the things about you if you don't even love certain things about you? If you haven't already, I would highly recommend you to read over the Self-Love chapter which goes over this in greater detail.

WHY AM I ALWAYS SINGLE?

A woman who has her eyes on the prize are never vibrationally in one place for too long. As we grow in learning to love ourselves, we constantly change and evolve to accommodate our new vibrations. Depending on your speed of vibrational change, you may find yourself always single, in short-lived relationships, relationships that never quite kick-off the ground, or a relationship that goes on for a while but has you so uncomfortable with yourself that you try to stay in it because you think the issue is you.

When we've come to a place of genuine desire to constantly advance, that is accompanied by ever-changing situations and yes, relationships. The key is to acknowledge and express gratitude in the qualities that make up who you are. This includes a strong desire to be the best and to achieve the best. Know who you are and embrace that. If a part of who you are involves an everlasting desire to get to know yourself, then you should embrace that. If a part of who you are involves becoming the best at what you do, embrace that as well.

A QUEEN MUST REIGN WITH A KING

A Queen that has realized her riches should protect that and her kingdom to her hearts content. As she governs her reality and leads her ambitions, she thrives in respect and love of herself. That said, a Queen that understands her worth and the worth of her Kingdom shall not compromise that for a matchless man. A Queen deserves a King.

A King who also understands he is an heir of abundance abounds in strength and love. A true King aims to protect and serve his kingdom and will put his kingdom before himself. He knows his worth and so exudes that worth through out his kingdom. He also leads his ambitions, governs his reality, and rules his happiness.

Queens, settle for nothing less than a King! A King who understands his value will value his Queen. A King who loves himself and has found a Queen who loves herself will effortlessly respect that. He would never do anything to take that light away because he knows what it feels like to have that light himself. A King who leads his ambitions will never stop the leadership of a Queen who leads hers. He will respect her decisions and support her throughout.

A King who rules his happiness will not try to rule the happiness of his Queen. Yes, you heard that correctly. A Queen should always rule her own happiness no matter what. She will always be the one to know what gives her joy. A King may learn over time what brings his Queen joy, but he will never fully know. Instead, a true King will give his Queen NEW happiness that will be added onto what currently brings her joy.

Where do you find such a king? Beloved, the more you continue to exude the qualities of a QUEEN, you will inevitably attract into your life a KING. However, you must continue to focus and work on yourself.

Love yourself effortlessly and so will your King.
Treat yourself splendidly and so will he.
Trust yourself and your ambitions, and so will he.
Respect yourself, and he will respect you.

Become what you want your King to be, and
your King will surely COME to be.

DAILY REMINDER

FALLING IN LOVE WITH YOU IS THE FIRST STEP TOWARD ATTRACTING GREATNESS

HOW TO KNOW WHEN YOU'VE MET YOUR KING

Ever meet a guy for the first time that you have an odd feeling about but continue to talk to out of curiosity? He says all the right things and you two have a few things in common & over time, you start to actually like him. Afterwards, you disregard your initial feelings & write it off as paranoia considering this guy isn't as bad as you thought.

From personal experience, after praying for discernment and intuition daily for 2 years, I now get incredibly strong vibes about every person I meet. Sometimes I wish it was all in my head, but it never seems to fail me. It's also something your mind truly cannot understand. It feels like a knowing, like an experience has already transpired between you and that person. When you feel it, you'll know.

The spirit knows what the mind cannot comprehend, beloved. I understand that it can be especially tough in your mid 20's when all of your friends are finding love and you're not. However, beware of the wolves in sheep clothing. It's easy to ignore the spirit during this stage in your life because we all want love and for the next guy we meet to be "the one". However, be reminded that as you constantly put out vibrations of who you are, many potential suitors who fit that description may come your way.

The key is to let things flow. When you've met someone new that you like, try not to obsess over them. Instead, continue to focus on what a healthy relationship full of love would feel like. Eventually, if that person isn't the one for you, they will drift away, back into the river of vibrational flow where they can be drawn to someone more suitable. A true connection between you and your vibrational match should flow effortlessly, so don't try to force something that isn't flowing. The last thing you want is to start hearing about this persons likes and dislikes and start changing yourself to fit the bill.

If you want to make the funnel of potential suitors smaller, continue to work on yourself to equate to greatness. It's not easy to miss yourself in male form. You would just know and can say...

"FINALLY, I'VE BEEN WAITING SO LONG FOR YOU TO ARRIVE!"

The downside is you may have to wait a bit longer for Mr. Perfect to arrive. But just imagine, right now as you wait for your King to come, he's been patiently waiting to meet his Queen too.

HOW-TO
ATTRACT YOUR IDEAL RELATIONSHIP

If you desire to be in a relationship that has certain qualities and makes you feel a certain way, write it down! Only you know you better than anyone else. Use the positive qualities of your past relationships as a way to carve out your ideal relationship. Don't you dare let anyone tell you your standards are too high. Especially when you've been working your butt off to become quite a catch!

THE LIST

What should this list look like? You can go as detailed or as broad as you'd like. However, many who have used this method advise being as detailed as possible. As it is true that we attract what we are, it does not mean that we will only attract a blue-eyed mate if we have blue eyes. Our vibrational match goes on feelings, so if you feel attracted to certain qualities about a man, you will end up attracting that inevitably. Just own up to it!

I personally highly recommend being as detailed as possible in this regard. The reason being is that when "Mr. Perfect" arrives, you will know without a shadow of a doubt that he came into your life because you willed for it to happen. This not only exercises your faith muscle, but will allow you to be more conscious of your abilities to attract anything you want in life.

There are a few things to consider in making your list:

Who you will be with

What will this person look like? What type of character are they? What do they like to do? Think back to your past relationships, what have you liked most about them? Really think about what you're attracted to. Make sure you feel really good while thinking about all of these attributes

Physically

Are they tall? What color are their eyes, does their smile make you melt? How do they typically like to dress?

This specific? Yes, because why not? Only you know what you're attracted to, and if being physically attracted to your partner is important, you have nothing to lose by envisioning what your perfect mate would look like.

Personality

What type of person are they? Are they funny? Do they love to learn? Are they as passionate and driven about business are you? Are they very family oriented? What about their morals? What are their plans for the future, do they want kids? Do they want to live in a big house in the suburbs, or a small apartment in the city?

What type of relationship you want

What does this relationship look like? Do you find you compliment each other well? Are you both supportive of each others individual dreams and goals? Do you two laugh often? Is your relationship filled with passion and adventure? Do the two of you just like to relax at home and watch movies?

What it will feel like

How does this relationship make you feel? Do you feel a sense of security? Do you trust them totally? Do you want to grow old with this person? Does time seem to stop when you're with them? Do they give you butterflies?

If you still don't know the answers to these questions, take a step back for a moment and really get to know yourself first. If you find it difficult to feel these feelings even in your head, you will find it difficult to feel it in reality. Understand your worth first. Understand the type of man who will fall for a gal like you. Get to know who this gal is, then go get your man!

AFFIRMATIONS
FOR ATTRACTING LOVE

I love myself unconditionally

I am deserving of love

I am worthy of love

I deserve a loving relationship

I radiate love

I am attracting a loving relationship into my life

My relationship is filled with joy, love, & security

My partner is everything I've ever wanted

I am grateful for my partner

My partner is faithful

I'm extremely attracted to my partner

My partner is extremely attracted to me

My relationship makes me happy

My relationship is filled with passion

My partner is incredibly romantic

I fall in love with my partner more and more everyday

I trust my partner totally

I am secure in my relationship

My relationship is very comfortable

I love being around my partner

I am equally yolked with my partner

BREAKUPS & INFIDELITY

THE PURPOSE OF RELATIONSHIPS

Since we attract into our lives what we are, we shouldn't forget to attribute that principle to our relationships. Any bond we establish with another human being has everything to do with who we were at the time of that encounter.

Top put things into perspective, imagine driving down a road at 50 mph. When looking to your sides, you can only see eye to eye with someone who also drives at or around 50mph. If you're lucky, you may be driving in the same direction. If you're determined to continue seeing eye to eye, you will force yourself to bend to their will. When they go right, you will, when they go left, you too.

It is understandable that seeing where your peers are going at times makes you want to go that way too. That said, when you've hit 50mph on the same road where you've met that new friend, it was because of your need or desire at the time to want to go where they were going.

Additionally, it's not only about wanting to bend to the vibrational will of your peers, but note the damage it's doing to you. You don't know when they're going to speed up or slow down, signal, switch lanes. You're causing yourself more harm trying to make something work with someone who has their own GPS dialed in.

Now, you can choose to keep this relationship that no longer serves a purpose, or you can choose to accelerate and drive wherever you please.

Beloved, know that when you've met someone who will be there long term, you won't need to look to your right or left to see if they're still there. You would simply go where you want to go and trust that that person will turn left when you do, and right when you do. This is because that person desires to be there too! It won't be because they want to see eye to eye with you, but they too are simply following the will of their heart.

Please don't be sad when someone you were once close with is close no more. When we lose one relationship, another one who shares our destination is driving right ahead.

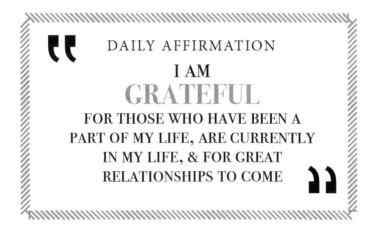

DAILY AFFIRMATION
I AM
GRATEFUL
FOR THOSE WHO HAVE BEEN A PART OF MY LIFE, ARE CURRENTLY IN MY LIFE, & FOR GREAT RELATIONSHIPS TO COME

WHY WOULD WE GET CHEATED ON?

We would never desire to be hurt by someone we love, so why does it happen? There are a few factors that can play into this.

One factor is "following your heart" which a majority of the time, is actually your ego. It at times so desperately wants to believe something that it ignores urges from your spirit saying "it's time to go". When you're determined to continue seeing eye to eye with someone, we may stay in and then create a bad relationship that no longer serves a purpose due to the vibrational imbalance. The key is knowing when to go the moment you feel a vibrational shift. Ask your spirit what course of action to take rather than remaining so attached to that person that you force yourself to stay in toxicity.

This can happen when we forget that the source of our love should come from within and not that person. The moment they start behaving differently, you may start questioning your own love and worth and will want to do all you can to get it back from them. This should never be the case.

Another is free will. You should remember that you cannot change someone no matter how much you believe. That said, no matter what type of vibes they may feel from you, they still have the ability to consciously decide to go against that and make their own choices. This definitely has absolutely nothing to do with you.

DON'T BE AFRAID TO LOSE A RELATIONSHIP. SOME PEOPLE ENTER OUR LIVES DURING A TIME OF NEED, AND LEAVE DURING A TIME OF GROWTH.

This may happen when that persons start to feel less of themselves & like they are not enough. In this case, they may seek gratification by connecting with someone else. This by the way in no way makes it right. However do not use this as an opportunity to try to fix them or disregard what has happened. Leave & give that person some time to re-align with who they were before they cheated. Reason being is that once a cheater has cheated, that thought about themselves is still active in their subconscious which means it will eventually re-manifest itself again if it is not corrected - they will cheat again.

All things considered, never seek a relationship to empower you or make you feel better or loved. You must have that love within yourself prior to meeting. Never be too attached to someone that you feel you can't live without them but it's rather that you choose to live a life with them.

You **ARE** enough.
You **ARE** all you need.
You **ARE** the source of your
happiness and joy.

Having a partner is merely the icing on the cake ;)

AFFIRMATIONS
FOR RENEWING LOVE

I am loved

I am whole

I am highly capable

I am beautiful

I am important

I am abundant

I am sufficient

4

PERSONAL DEVELOP- MENT

This chapter outlines personal growth. Since we achieve self-mastery through self-awareness, the more aware we become of our current path, the more control we gain over our future. These sections are ideal for anyone seeking self-improvement, spiritual growth, knowledge, and personal development.

PREP YOUR DAY

Every morning before I start my day I prep my mind. I do this by praying for four things that assist my productivity:

1. DIVINE INSPIRATION

Divine inspiration is essentially knowledge from a higher source. Because we have freewill, we are never subject to anything outside the physical that we do not wish to experience. This includes higher knowledge and understanding. If you wish to receive a little assistance in making decisions daily, try asking of this. We all essentially have this knowledge buried within us because we are an extension of All That Is and All That Ever Will Be. That said, if you want to attain your hearts desires quicker, it's best to receive direction from the very source that will bring these things into manifestation. Ask for this divine inspiration to excite and inspire ideas within you that will bring you closer to your goals.

2. DISCERNMENT

This is incredibly important, especially if you're in the business industry on your way to massive success. You will walk among many wolves in sheep's clothing and need to know who to associate with. There are many that may cross our paths that will speak with sweet words and great promises, however not all that come to us will come with good intentions. Ask for discernment in this regard to know who to trust, get close to, work with, and to expound your ideas.

THE SPIRIT KNOWS WHAT THE MIND CANNOT COMPREHEND

3. INTUITION

Ever meet someone for the first time and instantly get a feeling about them? Notice how a couple of seconds after, you start to ask your self questions as to why you feel that way accompanied by a rebuttal from your mind? They may speak sweet, and dress well - your inner gut says no but your mind says yes. Never ignore that first feeling, that is your intuition.

It should be understood that the mind can only correlate and put pieces together of a puzzle it has solved in the past. It knows what it has already experienced through stories of memory and attempts to output through association.

The spirit, however, knows every story ever told, every story that is soon to be created, and every story that will ever transpire. It is connected to every puzzle that has ever been created and has the solution to puzzles that have yet to be created.

As it is important for us to remain on our toes and use logic in most situations, let us never be deceived by the ego that still lurks around in our mind that likes to have the final say. The ego says, "This must be true because in the past, I've had a situation like this that resulted in XYZ."

Remember this when I tell you:

Each day is a new day! The past does not exist, what matters is now and moving forward.

This is why it is important to ask for the strengthening of your **intuition** and **discernmen**t daily. Outer influences and the ego of the mind come into play on a regular basis after each new experience we encounter. Let your spirit be your guide and usher you every day into the direction that you should go. Don't depend on me or anyone else to do that for you because you yourself have already been given the solutions to the problems in your life.

4. HUMILITY

Remaining humble is easier said than done, especially after each great accomplishment. Success is inevitable if you truly desire it, however let us never forget how we got there when we've finally reached the top. Never feel too big that you feel you cannot learn from someone else. Our journey is ongoing and expansive. Ask for humility to keep you grounded and unattached to the material possessions that you acquire in this life.

Remember this is not lip service. It will take less than 5 minutes to truly ask of this from your heart. The spirit works on feelings and vibrations that accompany your words and not just the words themselves. Keep this in mind when you ask for anything.

AFFIRMATIONS
FOR SPIRITUAL ATTUNEMENT

I am directed by the spirit

I am grateful for divine intervention

I invite divine intervention

I invite divine inspiration into my life

I perform daily actions that bring me closer to my goal

I discern between the good hearted and the ill will

My intuition grows stronger every day

I remain humble

I remain grateful

MAKING DECISIONS

When we put out thoughts & vibrations, they are accompanied by feeling. This feeling could be positive like joy or negative like fear. These feelings are like radio frequencies whereby the longer you tap into that frequency, the more that manifestation will be drawn to you.

Imagine that you are turning the dial on a radio and the closer you get to a station that actually has music playing, you begin to hear the sound. 104.0 faintly plays the sound you are looking for, but 104.3 hits the frequency just right where you're able to hear everything with clarity. Now imagine 104.3 is actually a feeling of joy and the music playing are the desires of your heart. In contrast, imagine 95.4 is a frequency of fear that only plays the sounds of things you don't want.

KNOW THE SOURCE OF RESISTANCE & PERSISTENCE

When there's an opportunity to make a decision in our life, we immediately get a feeling about it. There are two things that come into as a result; resistance or persistence. Do we move forward, or do we back away? When analyzing your options, before moving forward it's important to know which frequency you are making your decision from.

If your gut feeling persists "Yes", but theres also resistance saying "No", note what you're feeling that very moment. If fear accompanies the resistance - ignore the resistance. Why? Well this is because fear being on 95.4 only plays songs that you don't like and is causing interference. In other words, if you were to back away based on that frequency, you would be moving toward what you don't want. In contrast, if you feel you should back away, there is no fear present, but just a strong gut feeling saying "this isn't for me" - then listen to it!

It is also important to know the source of your persistence. When the universe is trying to deliver something to you, you will see or feel occurrences happening repeatedly. However, if the persistence is coming from you because you've got your mind set on it, check yourself! Are you feeling joy and peace while persisting or is it actually the fear of not having it that causes you to persist? If you're unsure, let it go for a season. If it returns in your life through divine will, you will certainly know!

This is why every morning you should renew your spirit to strengthen your discernment and intuition. Decisions will become easier once you know the source of resistance and persistence.

CO-CREATION

BEFORE YOU REALIZED YOU CREATED YOUR REALITY, YOU WERE CREATING EFFORTLESSLY - BEFORE YOU WERE CREATED, YOU WERE LOVED EFFORTLESSLY - AND IT WAS THROUGH THAT LOVE, YOU WERE CREATED.

The same DIVINE LOVE that created us only wants us to realize that we truly deserve to experience the fullness of joy. Look around at the beauty of the untouched world & the intricacies of beauty found in nature. Realize, **SOURCE** that created *that* is the same that resides within us.

How can we look at ourselves and see anything less than beauty when we were created with the essence of what beauty is? Why should you wake up with sadness and stress dreading another day that you must do what you have to just to live?

Life was granted to us as a gift, so, why should the life you experience be filled with nothing but grief when it was given to us by the **SOURCE** of joy?

The truth is, it should not. Understand that darkness is the absence of light. You can not add darkness into a room and have the room become dark. It's only when light is taken away that you're unable to see and experience its luminance.

You have all been given the opportunity to experience a beautiful life filled with love, joy, peace, happiness, growth, abundance - as long as you realize the source of that is the light you were created with.

If you are encountering struggle in your life right now, please know that you were never abandoned nor neglected. We are all given a choice to live life how we choose. If free will were not a universal law, we would have all been forced to experience goodness. But **DIVINE LOVE** does not force or impose. It desires us to be happy through our own choices and can only hope we find our way back to truth.

Your struggle-filled life stops the moment you realize that you were created to experience all **GOOD THINGS**. Now that you know, fix it.

YOUR WORDS HAVE THE POWER TO BUILD UP OR BREAK DOWN

As heirs of the Creator, we are made to be **builders** and not **breakers**. If all greatness comes from that which we were, then only great things should come from us. We build ourselves up with affirmations, words of inspiration, & encouragement. Yet, we can also break ourselves down by calling ourselves anything less than great during our times of weakness.

Do not call yourself stupid when you've done something wrong.
Do not call yourself lazy when you don't feel like doing something at that moment.
Do not call yourself incapable when you're unable to perform a task that you're not yet equipped to take it on.
Do not call yourself ugly when you are not looking your best.
Do not call yourself poor when your supply is running low.

Nothing good comes from those proclamations. Every time you call yourself that which you should never be, you become that which you were never made of.

To that respect, we should also take into account the words we speak onto others. In this era we, have the ability to reach massive amounts of people in a short period of time through technology. Because it is primarily through the form of text, we sit behind our computer screens and type away the first thing that comes to our mind without thinking of the ramifications.

I've been guilty of this, surely, we all have. However, remember that words we issue still hold the same power no matter what medium we send or receive them through. We are meant to build up, not break down. Let us be reminded that if we wouldn't say it to ourselves, not to say it to someone else. We forget at times and may think we're getting away with it because we're unable to see that persons face when they receive our message - but our actions are documented in every account.

We attract what we put out. To that regard, when we break someone down in one form, we will be broken down in another. Try building others up more. If you see a video you like, or an image someone posted, or a thread someone started - before you post a reply ask yourself "Is this going to build this person up, or break them down?". Make someones day through the power of your words.

AFFIRMATIONS
FOR PERSONAL DEVELOPMENT

I am a co-creator

I create my reality

I am in control

I am loved

I become a better me everyday

I am capable of achieving great things

My words are filled with love

I build others up

I fill my life with positivity

I fill my life with love

HOW-TO CREATE YOUR REALITY

#5

Just as we have different learning styles, there are different ways we find the easiest to actually immerse ourselves in our desired reality. If you're at that stage in your life where you know what you want in this life and are ready to put the pieces together, this chapter is for you.

VIRTUAL VISION BOARD

If you're more of a visual person and are always on the go, this method is for you. I've found it highly convenient to have a virtual vision board on me at all times. With Pinterest, this really is the best way to keep motivated on a regular basis. By having something on hand to remind you what you're working toward, you keep your positivity up and your eyes on the prize!

CREATE YOUR REALITY WITH
PINTEREST

If you're unfamiliar, Pinterest is a social media platform that allows you to assemble a collection of images and links that you've gathered from around the web. You can create many different boards that you theme yourself and pin whatever interests you.

On Pinterest, I have a handful of secret boards that are meant for my eyes only. (Tip: You should always keep your goals and progress to yourself!) You can utilize this method by making private boards for each area of your life that you'd like to come to fruition. Label each image as if these things are already here rather than "will be" here and only pin things that truly give you a feeling of joy. Below are some examples of the type of boards you may want to create to visualize your ideal lifestyle.

MY HEALTH

If you're working on a slimmer or more toned body, pin photos of people who are in shape and add affirmations to the caption. Include words like:

"I love how in shape I am!"
"I have so much energy"
"My body is incredible!"

Write out what you would like to feel as a result of what you see in the image. Claim it as if it has already happened. Perhaps you're trying to eat healthier. In that case, consider pinning photos of delicious meals that you'd love to be able to cook. Caption them with things like:

"I love eating healthy."
"Everything I eat only makes me stronger, more healthy, and more energized!"

MY WEALTH

As mentioned in the chapter about wealth and prosperity, money will flow to fulfill a purpose that demands the amount. If you want to attract a more abundant life, visualize what an abundant life would look and feel like to you. You can do this by illustrat-

ing what you plan on doing with your wealth.
Wealth comes in many forms. It can be expressed in the form of expensive items like cars, homes, luxury products. Or, it can be experienced in the form of achievements like travel, attending events, having a successful business, or simply freedom.

When you gather images, remember always to caption them in the present tense with:

"My car is so beautiful!"
"I just bought my dream house today,
it's everything I could have ever wanted!"
"I am able to travel wherever I want,
whenever I want"
"I own a successful business"
"I feel a sense of accomplishment every day!"

MY LOVE LIFE
Don't be bashful with this. Your board is private so go wild with your imagination! As noted in the Attracting Love chapter, the more descriptive, the better!

Find pictures of people you find attractive, photos of romantic get-aways, couples holding hands or kissing. Become enveloped in the idea of being in a real loving relationship. What does security look like to you? What about trust, joy, and passion?

Add captions to your pins that describe what you want in a relationship:

"My relationship is filled with so much
love and passion!"
"I feel so comfortable around my lover,
they're everything I've ever wanted!"

As the days go on, anything you see that excites your spirit, pin it and claim it. You'll be very....VERY surprised to come back to these boards months from now at how many have shown up in your life!

AS IF
JOURNALING

As I've mentioned in a previous chapter:
"...the universe cannot differentiate between a real memory or a fabricated one. It goes on how you felt and reacted as a result of visual experience."

To reiterate, focusing on memories of events that have already happened is the equivalent to focusing on events that haven't happened yet. That said, if you're able to immerse yourself deeply into a fabricated experience in your mind with what you visualize, experience, and FEEL as a result of that, you can and WILL attract more of the same.

As If Journaling is a method where you write your life experiences AS IF it's already happened. This is an opportunity to be as descriptive and detailed as possible and write your own adventure! What makes this method so effective in evoking emotion is that it takes you through your desired experience as if you're recalling a memory. Try not to overwhelm yourself - you don't have to write an entire story. Just write as if you were writing in your diary telling yourself about your day - only, make it up.

Take it one experience at a time. Example:

> *Today I woke up at 5am to get ready for my flight to Dubai. I have some business to attend to while I'm there but I'm mostly looking forward to the shopping and exploring the city! I was so excited about the trip I had packed a week in advance. I had so many shoes to choose from, it was hard to choose which ones to bring!*

Make sure that everything you're typing up or writing down makes you feel good. Feel it as if it's happening, like really happening. Be as descriptive as possible. Explain the sights, sounds, what you're wearing, what you see, what you smell, the people you meet, etc.

I've used this and still do. You'll be very surprised when you return to your journal to see how many of your experiences happened exactly as you wrote it.

Ready to start journaling?

In this physical copy of my book, I've created extra pages at the very end for you to begin journaling right away! Considering it's best to get your thoughts down at the peak of your motivation and excitement, what better way to do that than after reading all of this motivational content. After you've used all of the pages I've provided in this book, I would encourage you to get another journal to create a routine of envisioning your desired reality. Trust me, you won't regret it!

GOOGLE ADS

Did you know that messages we receive subliminally have more of an affect on what we attract than the things we consciously see? This is because whatever you set into your subconscious mind determines your vibration, and whatever you vibrate - you attract. With this method, we will immerse ourselves in our desired reality by skipping the step of repetitive conscious thinking and go straight to the subconscious level.

Do you notice what ads are shown to you on websites you browse? Chances are - probably not. Truth is, over time ad blindness has increased to over 86% and most can't remember the last text or image advertisement they viewed on the page before. However, just because you don't remember doesn't mean your subconscious mind doesn't. This is where you need to take control!

If you desire financial success, another way to get it is to tell the universe what you plan on doing with that money. The truth is, the universe doesn't really see a $$ amount because money is useless if it is not being spent. To reiterate, $1 is synonymous to $1,000,000 so long as the purpose demands the amount, so don't limit yourself. There is no such thing as "too much", because I mean, aren't you worth it?

If you have targeted ads enabled by google, (the most probable case) you will most likely see ads of things you've recently browsed. The most effective way to have those ads show what you want is to shop, shop, shop; add them to cart but just don't check out! For example, perhaps you want a dream home and know exactly how you're going to decorate it, well, start shopping for furniture! Make sure what you're looking at really excites you and is something you'd love. Get into the feeling of "I'm furnishing my new home" and don't you dare for a second cheat yourself by looking at the price.

You can do this with cars, homes, vacation destinations, apparel, office spaces, furniture, etc… whatever you can think of - go crazy! You should begin to receive ads that have to do with what you were browsing for.

Try to do this every couple of days. This will assist you in attracting your desires through out the day without having to think about it.

YOUR SPACE

....

As mentioned in the guide for creating your reality with Google Ads:

"...messages we receive subliminally have more of an affect on what we attract than the things we consciously see...whatever you set into your subconscious mind determines your vibration, and whatever you vibrate you attract."

That considered, it's important to make sure the things we are surrounded by agree with the mindset we're trying to achieve. If you find it hard to focus or get creative in your work space, it may be a good idea to re-examine what your mind is picking up from your surroundings.

Even if you're looking at a screen all day, there are still objects in your background (that reside in your office) that your subconscious mind picks up. If your subconscious-mind is picking up something that isn't in agreement with what you're trying to do, it can cause some interference.

Try looking at your desk, are there things that shouldn't be there? Are there colors that put you off? Perhaps there are objects there from someone you no longer speak to? Get rid of the things that represent a time in your life where you USED to be.

After you've decluttered, consider adding things to your office that illustrate where you aim to be. If you're looking to get a new car, get a car catalog and put it on your desk. Consider adding a vision board to a wall that you face often while sitting at your desk. Your subconscious mind will pick these things up while you're working and should motivate you to keep working!

HAPPY SPACE
=
HAPPY FACE

Take some time today to really change some things around till everything feels right. Make sure you feel joy while getting rid of something, and joy when adding something. You should feel a sigh of relief like you can breathe again once your surroundings are in agreement with your vision.

HAVE YOU RECEIVED CLARITY?

We've arrived at the end of this book! I am truly happy for you and grateful that you took the time to read it. As I stated in the beginning of this book, utilize the words written here as prescription medication. Take it when you need to and really focus on the areas that you'd like to have improved in your life.

You've already taken a great step in the right direction by making the sacrifice of purchasing this book. This displays that at some level, you're ready to make more sacrifices to truly start seeing change in your life. I'm excited for you!

I have been exactly where you are right now. That place where you've come to realize that you deserve more out of life. More than what you're currently experiencing, more than what your friends or family think you're capable of. You ARE more, you DESERVE more.

WHO AM I

If you're wondering a bit about the woman behind this book, I'll tell you. I'm an Entrepreneur, Webpreneur to be exact, in my late 20's, who has been fortunate enough to have grasped unto the concept of being the creator of my own reality. Although for nearly 10 years I've been self-taught and self-employed in the web industry, it wasn't until recently that I decided to take full control of my life.

We're all aware that theory and practice are two completely different things, and as much as you may have heard by numerous millionaires and entrepreneurs that thoughts create reality, how many have actually taken the time to practice what was preached?

The moment I began to apply many different methods of manifesting abundance and financial stability into my life was the moment it actually started to change.

December 2014, I decided to start an account on Instagram called "Minding Her Business". Initially, I planned on posting a few motivational quotes here and there to inspire women. However, what intended to be a quotes page actually ended up becoming an Instagram blog where I shared long captions of thoughts & insight on what I had learned about life and success.

I've always wanted to teach others what I've learned but always felt I wouldn't have anything valuable to share unless I became a millionaire myself - how wrong I was... I realized that success, no matter how big or small, is still success. I learned how to get exactly what I wanted, when I wanted, and the methods I've used to get there itself is something worth sharing. Although I certainly have bigger goals now, I'm definitely on my way there and aim to share my methods of motivation, inspiration, and guidance to other women that aim for that same freedom.

YOUR STORY

Now it's your turn to start creating an extraordinary life that you deserve. Given all that you've learned from this book, don't hold back on writing down what you really want. Make sure that every affirmation, sentence, and proclamation creates such an overwhelming feeling of joy within you. This is YOUR life story, make it a best seller!

A PRAYER OF BLESSING

May your heart be forever filled with desire.
May your light of positivity remain bright.
Be abundant in joy, health, prosperity, wisdom, faith,
family and love.
Be at peace with your decisions, actions, and feelings.
Be forever blessed and focused on the things that
bring you joy.

A FABULOUS LIFE

BY

_____

SIGN YOUR NAME

HOW-TO

You can use this portion of the journal to write from an "As If" perspective or the present tense. As long you are writing down pleasurable, joyful experiences, it does not matter if they have happened or not.

EXAMPLE:

I had the most amazing day today! I just landed an amazing deal with a high paying client that's really going to put my company on the map!

....

....

....

....

CONVERGE YOUR REALITY : Because we perpetuate that which
we constantly focus on or "highlight", the best way to break a habit of
negative thinking is by featuring thoughts of the opposite. In this section
of your journal, you are encouraged to highlight the positive aspects of
your day that induce positive feeling.

POSITIVE CONVERGENCE

I felt a moment of reassurance when... my client called to
confirm that they would be sending payment by the end of this
week.

I felt joy when... this guy held the door open for me today and
gave me a nice smile :)

It gave me a sense of peace when... I finally wrote down my
entire goals for this week!

I felt abundant today when... I was able to pay my car bill and
still had money left over to pay for the things I need.

....

....

....

....

....

....

....

....

POSITIVE CONVERGENCE

....

I felt a moment of reassurance when...

....

I felt joy when...

....

It gave me a sense of peace when...

....

I felt abundant today when...

....

....

TODAY IS

___ / ___ / ___

....

....

....

....

....

....

....

....

POSITIVE CONVERGENCE

I felt a moment of reassurance when...

I felt joy when...

It gave me a sense of peace when...

I felt abundant today when...

TODAY IS

___ / ___ / ___

....

....

....

....

....

....

....

....

....

POSITIVE CONVERGENCE

I felt a moment of reassurance when...

....

I felt joy when...

....

It gave me a sense of peace when...

....

I felt abundant today when...

....

....

TODAY IS

___ / ___ / ___

....

....

....

....

....

....

....

....

POSITIVE CONVERGENCE

....

I felt a moment of reassurance when...

....

I felt joy when...

....

It gave me a sense of peace when...

....

I felt abundant today when...

....

....

TODAY IS

_____ / _____ / _____

....

....

....

....

....

....

....

....

....

POSITIVE CONVERGENCE

I felt a moment of reassurance when...

I felt joy when...

It gave me a sense of peace when...

I felt abundant today when...

TODAY IS

___ / ___ / ___

....

....

....

....

....

....

....

....

POSITIVE CONVERGENCE

....

I felt a moment of reassurance when...

....

I felt joy when...

....

It gave me a sense of peace when...

....

I felt abundant today when...

....

....

TODAY IS

___ / ___ / ___

....

....

....

....

....

....

....

....

POSITIVE CONVERGENCE

I felt a moment of reassurance when...

I felt joy when...

It gave me a sense of peace when...

I felt abundant today when...

TODAY IS

___ / ___ / ___

....

....

....

....

....

....

....

....

POSITIVE CONVERGENCE

....

I felt a moment of reassurance when...

....

I felt joy when...

....

It gave me a sense of peace when...

....

I felt abundant today when...

....

....

TODAY IS

___ / ___ / ___

....

....

....

....

....

....

....

....

....

....

POSITIVE CONVERGENCE

....

I felt a moment of reassurance when…

....

I felt joy when…

....

It gave me a sense of peace when…

....

I felt abundant today when…

....

....

TODAY IS

____ / ____ / ____

....

....

....

....

....

....

....

....

POSITIVE CONVERGENCE

....

I felt a moment of reassurance when...

....

....

I felt joy when...

....

....

It gave me a sense of peace when...

....

....

I felt abundant today when...

....

....

....

....

....

....

....

....

....

....

POSITIVE CONVERGENCE

....

I felt a moment of reassurance when...

....

I felt joy when...

....

It gave me a sense of peace when...

....

I felt abundant today when...

....

....

TODAY IS

____ / ____ / ____

....

....

....

....

....

....

....

....

POSITIVE CONVERGENCE

....

I felt a moment of reassurance when...

....

I felt joy when...

....

It gave me a sense of peace when...

....

I felt abundant today when...

....

....

TODAY IS

___ / ___ / ___

....

....

....

....

....

....

....

....

....

POSITIVE CONVERGENCE

....

I felt a moment of reassurance when...

....

I felt joy when...

....

It gave me a sense of peace when...

....

I felt abundant today when...

....

....

TODAY IS

___ / ___ / ___

....

....

....

....

....

....

....

....

POSITIVE CONVERGENCE

....

I felt a moment of reassurance when...

....

I felt joy when...

....

It gave me a sense of peace when...

....

I felt abundant today when...

....

....

TODAY IS

___ / ___ / ___

....

....

....

....

....

....

....

....

POSITIVE CONVERGENCE

I felt a moment of reassurance when...

....

I felt joy when...

....

It gave me a sense of peace when...

....

I felt abundant today when...

....

....

TODAY IS

___ / ___ / ___

POSITIVE CONVERGENCE

I felt a moment of reassurance when...

I felt joy when...

It gave me a sense of peace when...

I felt abundant today when...

TODAY IS

___ / ___ / ___

....

....

....

....

....

....

....

....

POSITIVE CONVERGENCE

....

I felt a moment of reassurance when...

....

I felt joy when...

....

It gave me a sense of peace when...

....

I felt abundant today when...

....

....

TODAY IS

___ / ___ / ___

....

....

....

....

....

....

....

....

....

POSITIVE CONVERGENCE

I felt a moment of reassurance when...

....

I felt joy when...

....

It gave me a sense of peace when...

....

I felt abundant today when...

....

....

TODAY IS

___ / ___ / ___

....

....

....

....

....

....

....

....

POSITIVE CONVERGENCE

....

I felt a moment of reassurance when...

....

I felt joy when...

....

It gave me a sense of peace when...

....

I felt abundant today when...

....

....

TODAY IS

___ / ___ / ___

....

....

....

....

....

....

....

....

POSITIVE CONVERGENCE

....

I felt a moment of reassurance when...

....

I felt joy when...

....

It gave me a sense of peace when...

....

I felt abundant today when...

....

....

TODAY IS

___ / ___ / ___

....

....

....

....

....

....

....

....

POSITIVE CONVERGENCE

....

I felt a moment of reassurance when...

....

I felt joy when...

....

It gave me a sense of peace when...

....

I felt abundant today when...

....

....

TODAY IS

___ / ___ / ___

....

....

....

....

....

....

....

....

POSITIVE CONVERGENCE

I felt a moment of reassurance when...

I felt joy when...

It gave me a sense of peace when...

I felt abundant today when...

TODAY IS

____ / ____ / ____

....

....

....

....

....

....

....

....

POSITIVE CONVERGENCE

....

I felt a moment of reassurance when...

....

I felt joy when...

....

It gave me a sense of peace when...

....

I felt abundant today when...

....

....

TODAY IS

___ / ___ / ___

....

....

....

....

....

....

....

....

POSITIVE CONVERGENCE

....

I felt a moment of reassurance when...

....

I felt joy when...

....

It gave me a sense of peace when...

....

I felt abundant today when...

....

....

Made in the USA
Middletown, DE
07 January 2019